thoughtful SHAWLS

For relaxing with your thoughts or a good book, you'll want one of these generously sized shawls. Each is easy to crochet in stripes, granny squares, or motifs.

LEISURE ARTS, INC.
Maumelle, Arkansas

Granny Square Shawl

EASY

Finished Size: Outer Edges - 49" (124.5 cm) long; Inner Edges - 25" (63.5 cm) long

SHOPPING LIST

Yarn (Medium Weight) MEDIUM 4
[3.5 ounces, 208 yards (100 grams, 190 meters) per skein**]**:

- ☐ MC (Grey) - 4 skeins
- ☐ Color A (Off White) - 1 skein
- ☐ Color B (Dk Blue) - 1 skein
- ☐ Color C (Gold) - 1 skein
- ☐ Color D (Rose) - 1 skein

Crochet Hook

- ☐ Size J (6 mm) **or** size needed for gauge

GAUGE INFORMATION

Back = 23" (58.5 cm) square
Gauge Swatch:
6" (15.25 cm) square
Work same as Back through Rnd 4: 48 dc and 16 sps.

BACK

With Color C, ch 3; join with slip st to form a ring.

Rnd 1 (Right side)**:** Ch 3 **(counts as first dc, now and throughout)**, 2 dc in ring, ch 3, (3 dc in ring, ch 3) 3 times; join with slip st to first dc: 12 dc and 4 ch-3 sps.

Note: Loop a short piece of yarn around any stitch to mark Rnd 1 as **right** side.

Rnd 2: Slip st in next 2 dc and in next ch-3 sp, ch 3, (2 dc, ch 3, 3 dc) in same sp, ch 1, ★ (3 dc, ch 3, 3 dc) in next ch-3 sp, ch 1; repeat from ★ 2 times **more**; join with slip st to first dc, finish off: 24 dc and 8 sps.

Rnd 3: With **right** side facing, join Color A with dc in any corner ch-3 sp ***(see Joining With Dc, page 29)***; (2 dc, ch 3, 3 dc) in same sp, ch 1, 3 dc in next ch-1 sp, ch 1, ★ (3 dc, ch 3, 3 dc) in next corner ch-3 sp, ch 1, 3 dc in next ch-1 sp, ch 1; repeat from ★ 2 times **more**; join with slip st to first dc: 36 dc and 12 sps.

Rnd 4: Slip st in next 2 dc and in next corner ch-3 sp, ch 3, (2 dc, ch 3, 3 dc) in same sp, ch 1, (3 dc in next ch-1 sp, ch 1) twice, ★ (3 dc, ch 3, 3 dc) in next corner ch-3 sp, ch 1, (3 dc in next ch-1 sp, ch 1) twice; repeat from ★ 2 times **more**; join with slip st to first dc, finish off: 48 dc and 16 sps.

Rnd 5: With **right** side facing, join Color D with dc in any corner ch-3 sp; (2 dc, ch 3, 3 dc) in same sp, ch 1, ★ (3 dc in next ch-1 sp, ch 1) across to next corner ch-3 sp, (3 dc, ch 3, 3 dc) in corner sp, ch 1; repeat from ★ 2 times **more**, (3 dc in next ch-1 sp, ch 1) across; join with slip st to first dc: 60 dc and 20 sps.

Rnd 6: Slip st in next 2 dc and in next corner ch-3 sp, ch 3, (2 dc, ch 3, 3 dc) in same sp, ch 1, ★ (3 dc in next ch-1 sp, ch 1) across to next corner ch-3 sp, (3 dc, ch 3, 3 dc) in corner sp, ch 1; repeat from ★ 2 times **more**, (3 dc in next ch-1 sp, ch 1) across; join with slip st to first dc, finish off: 72 dc and 24 sps.

Rnds 7-18: Repeat Rnds 5 and 6, 6 times working in the following color sequence: 2 Rnds **each**, Color A, Color C, Color A, Color D, Color A, Color C: 216 dc and 72 sps.

FIRST EXTENSION

Row 1: With **right** side facing, join MC with dc in any corner ch-3 sp; 2 dc in same sp, ch 1, (3 dc in next ch-1 sp, ch 1) across to next corner ch-3 sp, 3 dc in corner sp, place a marker around same corner sp for Second Extension placement: 57 dc and 18 ch-1 sps.

Row 2: Ch 4 **(counts as first dc plus ch 1)**, turn; (3 dc in next ch-1 sp, ch 1) across to last 3 dc, skip next 2 dc, dc in last dc: 56 dc and 19 ch-1 sps.

Row 3: Ch 3, turn; 2 dc in next ch-1 sp, (ch 1, 3 dc in next ch-1 sp) across, leave last dc unworked: 57 dc and 18 ch-1 sps.

Rows 4-39: Repeat Rows 2 and 3, 18 times: 57 dc and 18 ch-1 sps.

Finish off.

SECOND EXTENSION

Row 1: With **right** side facing, join MC with dc in marked corner sp, do **not** remove marker; 2 dc in same sp, ch 1, (3 dc in next ch-1 sp, ch 1) across to next corner ch-3 sp, 3 dc in corner sp: 57 dc and 18 ch-1 sps.

Complete same as First Extension.

EDGING

Rnd 1: With **right** side facing, join Color B with sc in marked sp (between First & Second Extensions) ***(see Joining With Sc, page 29)***, remove marker; † 2 sc in end of each row across Extension; working in sts and sps across last row of Extension, 3 sc in first st, sc in each st and in each sp across to last st, 3 sc in last st; 2 sc in end of each row across opposite side of Extension †; (sc in next sp and in next 3 dc) across to corner ch-3 sp on Back, 5 sc in corner sp, (sc in next 3 dc and in next sp) across to next Extension; repeat from † to † once; join with slip st to first sc: 620 sc.

Rnd 2: Ch 1, turn; sc in each sc around working 3 sc in center sc of each corner; join with slip st to first sc: 630 sc.

Rnd 3: Ch 2, do **not** turn; slip st in second ch from hook, skip next sc, ★ slip st in next sc, ch 2, slip st in second ch from hook, skip next sc; repeat from ★ around; join with slip st at base of beginning ch-2, finish off.

Hudson Shawl

EASY

Finished Size:
22" high x 53½" long
(56 cm x 136 cm)

SHOPPING LIST

Yarn (Medium Weight) MEDIUM 4
[6 ounces, 315 yards
(170.1 grams, 288 meters)
per skein]:

- ☐ MC (Off White) - 3 skeins
- ☐ Color A (Green) - 1 skein
- ☐ Color B (Red) - 1 skein
- ☐ Color C (Yellow) - 1 skein
- ☐ Color D (Black) - 1 skein

Crochet Hook

- ☐ Size L (8 mm)
  or size needed for gauge

Shawl is worked holding two strands of yarn held together throughout. Wind Colors A-D into two balls as well as the third skein of MC.

GAUGE INFORMATION

Holding two strands together,
9 sc = 4" (10 cm);
8 rows = 3" (7.5 cm)

Gauge Swatch: 4" wide x 3" high
(10 cm x 7.5 cm)

Holding two strands of MC together, ch 10.

Row 1: Sc in second ch from hook and in each ch across: 9 sc.

Rows 2-8: Ch 1, turn; sc in each sc across.

Finish off.

BODY

Holding two strands of MC together, ch 121.

Row 1 (Right side)**:** Sc in second ch from hook and in each ch across: 120 sc.

Note: Loop a short piece of yarn around any stitch to mark Row 1 as **right** side.

Rows 2-8: Ch 1, turn; sc in each sc across; at end of Row 8, change to Color A in last sc *(Fig. 2a, page 30)*; cut MC.

Rows 9-14: Ch 1, turn; sc in each sc across; at end of Row 14, change to MC in last sc; cut Color A.

Rows 15-20: Ch 1, turn; sc in each sc across; at end of Row 20, change to Color B in last sc; cut MC.

Rows 21-26: Ch 1, turn; sc in each sc across; at end of Row 26, change to MC in last sc; cut Color B.

Rows 27-32: Ch 1, turn; sc in each sc across; at end of Row 32, change to Color C in last sc; cut MC.

Rows 33-38: Ch 1, turn; sc in each sc across; at end of Row 38, change to MC in last sc; cut Color C.

Row 39-44: Ch 1, turn; sc in each sc across; at end of Row 44, change to Color D in last sc; cut MC.

Rows 45-50: Ch 1, turn; sc in each sc across; at end of Row 50, change to MC in last sc; cut Color D.

Rows 51-58: Ch 1, turn; sc in each sc across.

Finish off.

EDGING

With **right** side facing and working in sts across Row 58, join Color D with sc in first sc *(see Joining with Sc, page 29)*; 2 sc in same st, † (ch 1, skip next st, sc in next st) across to last st, 3 sc in last st, ch 1; working in end of rows, skip first 2 rows, (sc in next row, ch 1, skip next row) across †; working in free loops of beginning ch *(Fig. 1, page 30)*, 3 sc in first ch, repeat from † to † once; join with slip st to first sc, finish off.

Stripes Stole

EASY

Finished Size: 23" high x 68" long (58.5 cm x 172.5 cm) (including fringe)

SHOPPING LIST

Yarn (Medium Weight) MEDIUM 4
[3.5 ounces, 147 yards (100 grams, 134 meters) per skein]:

☐ 8 skeins self-striping yarn

Crochet Hook

☐ Size K (6.5 mm) **or** size needed for gauge

GAUGE INFORMATION

Back = 23" (58.5 cm) square

Gauge Swatch:
6" (15.25 cm) square

Work same as Back through Rnd 4: 48 dc and 16 sps.

BACK

Ch 3; join with slip st to form a ring.

Rnd 1 (Right side)**:** Ch 3 **(counts as first dc, now and throughout)**, 2 dc in ring, ch 3, (3 dc in ring, ch 3) 3 times; join with slip st to first dc: 12 dc and 4 ch-3 sps.

Note: Loop a short piece of yarn around any stitch to mark Rnd 1 as **right** side.

Rnd 2: Slip st in next 2 dc and in next ch-3 sp, ch 3, (2 dc, ch 3, 3 dc) in same sp, ch 1, ★ (3 dc, ch 3, 3 dc) in next ch-3 sp, ch 1; repeat from ★ 2 times **more**; join with slip st to first dc: 24 dc and 8 sps.

Rnd 3: Slip st in next 2 dc and in next corner ch-3 sp, ch 3, (2 dc, ch 3, 3 dc) in same sp, ch 1, 3 dc in next ch-1 sp, ch 1, ★ (3 dc, ch 3, 3 dc) in next corner ch-3 sp, ch 1, 3 dc in next ch-1 sp, ch 1; repeat from ★ 2 times **more**; join with slip st to first dc: 36 dc and 12 sps.

Rnds 4-18: Slip st in next 2 dc and in next corner ch-3 sp, ch 3, (2 dc, ch 3, 3 dc) in same sp, ch 1, ★ (3 dc in next ch-1 sp, ch 1) across to next corner ch-3 sp, (3 dc, ch 3, 3 dc) in corner sp, ch 1; repeat from ★ 2 times **more**, (3 dc in next ch-1 sp, ch 1) across; join with slip st to first dc: 216 dc and 72 sps.

Do **not** finish off.

FIRST EXTENSION

Row 1: Slip st in next 2 dc and in next corner ch-3 sp, ch 3, 2 dc in same sp, ch 1, (3 dc in next ch-1 sp, ch 1) across to next corner ch-3 sp, 3 dc in corner sp: 57 dc and 18 ch-1 sps.

Row 2: Ch 4 **(counts as first dc plus ch 1, now and throughout)**, turn; (3 dc in next ch-1 sp, ch 1) across to last 3 dc, skip next 2 dc, dc in last dc: 56 dc and 19 ch-1 sps.

Row 3: Ch 3, turn; 2 dc in next ch-1 sp, (ch 1, 3 dc in next ch-1 sp) across leave last dc unworked: 57 dc and 18 ch-1 sps.

Row 4: Ch 4, turn; (3 dc in next ch-1 sp, ch 1) across to last 3 dc, skip next 2 dc, dc in last dc: 56 dc and 19 ch-1 sps.

Rows 5-30: Repeat Rows 3 and 4, 13 times.

Crochet Fringe: Ch 20, turn; skip next ch-1 sp, slip st in next dc, ★ ch 20, skip next dc, slip st in next dc, ch 20, skip next ch-1 sp, slip st in next dc; repeat from ★ across; finish off.

SECOND EXTENSION

Row 1: With **right** side of opposite side of Back facing, join yarn with slip st in first unworked corner ch-3 sp; ch 3, 2 dc in same sp, ch 1, (3 dc in next ch-1 sp, ch 1) across to next corner ch-3 sp, 3 dc in corner sp: 57 dc and 18 ch-1 sps.

Complete same as First Extension.

Meditation Shawl

EASY

Finished Size: 19" high x 58" wide (48.5 cm x 147.5 cm)

SHOPPING LIST

Yarn (Medium Weight) MEDIUM 4
[3.5 ounces, 147 yards (100 grams, 134 meters) per skein]:

- ☐ MC (Burgundy) - 4 skeins
- ☐ CC (Rose) - 3 skeins

Crochet Hooks

- ☐ Size J (6 mm) **and**
- ☐ Size K (6.5 mm)
  or sizes needed for gauge

GAUGE INFORMATION

With larger size hook,
in (sc, dc) pattern, 13 sts and 12 rows = 5" (12.75 cm)
13 sc = 5" (12.75 cm); 12 rows = 3½" (9 cm)

Gauge Swatch:
6" wide x 2½" high (15.25 cm x 6.25 cm)
With larger size hook and MC, ch 17.
Work same as Body for 6 rows: 16 sts.
Finish off.

BODY

With larger size hook and MC, ch 151.

Row 1 (Right side)**:** Sc in second ch from hook, dc in next ch, (sc in next ch, dc in next ch) across: 150 sts.

Note: Loop a short piece of yarn around any stitch to mark Row 1 as **right** side.

Rows 2-11: Ch 1, turn; sc in first dc, dc in next sc, (sc in next dc, dc in next sc) across.

Row 12: Ch 1, turn; sc in first dc, dc in next sc, (sc in next dc, dc in next sc) across changing to CC in last dc ***(Fig. 2b, page 30)***, do **not** cut MC.

Dropped colors will be held **loosely** at the end of the rows.

Row 13: Ch 1, turn; sc in each st across.

Rnd 14: Ch 1, turn; sc in each sc across changing to MC in last sc *(Fig. 2a, page 30)*, do **not** cut CC.

Row 15: Ch 1, turn; sc in each sc across.

Row 16: Ch 1, turn; sc in each sc across changing to CC in last sc, do **not** cut MC.

Rows 17-24: Repeat Rows 13-16 twice; at end of Row 24, cut MC.

Rows 25-36: Ch 1, turn; sc in first st, dc in next st, (sc in next st, dc in next st) across; at end of Row 36, change to MC in last dc, do **not** cut CC.

Row 37: Ch 1, turn; sc in each st across.

Row 38: Ch 1, turn; sc in each sc across changing to CC in last sc, do **not** cut MC.

Row 39: Ch 1, turn; sc in each sc across.

Row 40: Ch 1, turn; sc in each sc across changing to MC in last sc, do **not** cut CC.

Rows 41-48: Repeat Rows 37-40 twice; at end of Row 48, cut CC.

Neck Border

Row 1: Ch 1, turn; sc in each sc across.

Rows 2-9: Ch 1, turn; sc in Back Loop Only of each sc across *(Fig. A)*; at end of Row 9, do **not** finish off.

Fig. A

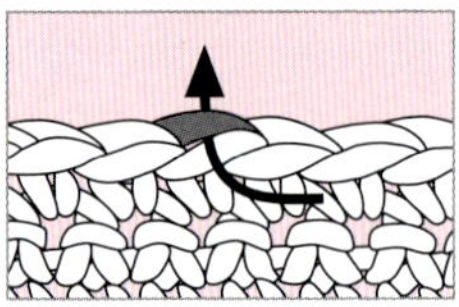

EDGING

Change to smaller size hook.

Ch 1, do **not** turn; sc evenly across end of rows; working in free loops of beginning ch *(Fig. 1, page 30)*, 3 sc in first ch, sc in each ch across to ch at base of last sc, 3 sc in ch; sc evenly across end of rows; finish off.

Patchwork Shawl

EASY +

Finished Size: 21" high x 61" wide (53.5 cm x 155 cm)

SHOPPING LIST

Yarn (Medium Weight) MEDIUM 4
[5 ounces, 251 yards (142 grams, 230 meters) per skein]:

- ☐ MC (Grey) - 3 skeins
- ☐ Color A (Green) - 2 skeins
- ☐ Color B (Gold) - 1 skein
- ☐ Color C (Lt Grey) - 1 skein

Crochet Hook

- ☐ Size J (6 mm) **or** size needed for gauge

Additional Supplies

- ☐ Yarn needle

GAUGE INFORMATION

Each Square = 5" (12.75 cm)
Gauge Swatch: 4" (10 cm) circumference
Work same as Solid Square through Rnd 3: 36 dc and 12 ch-1 sps.

STITCH GUIDE

TREBLE CROCHET *(abbreviated tr)*
YO twice, insert hook in sp indicated, YO and pull up a loop (4 loops on hook), (YO and draw through 2 loops on hook) 3 times.

SOLID SQUARE (Make 24)

With MC, ch 3; join with slip st to form a ring.

Rnd 1 (Right side)**:** Ch 3 **(counts as first dc, now and throughout)**, 11 dc in ring; join with slip st to first dc: 12 dc.

Note: Loop a short piece of yarn around any stitch to mark Rnd 1 as **right** side.

Rnd 2: Ch 4 **(counts as first dc plus ch 1, now and throughout)**, (dc in next dc, ch 1) 11 times; join with slip st to first dc: 12 dc and 12 ch-1 sps.

Rnd 3: Ch 3, (dc, ch 1, dc) in next ch-1 sp, ★ dc in next dc, (dc, ch 1, dc) in next ch-1 sp; repeat from ★ around; join with slip st to first dc: 36 dc and 12 ch-1 sps.

Rnd 4: Slip st in next dc and in next ch-1 sp, ch 7 **(counts as first tr plus ch 3, now and throughout)**, tr in same sp, skip next dc, dc in next 2 dc, hdc in next ch-1 sp, sc in next 3 dc, hdc in next ch-1 sp, dc in next 2 dc, skip next dc, ★ (tr, ch 3, tr) in next ch-1 sp, skip next dc, dc in next 2 dc, hdc in next ch-1 sp, sc in next 3 dc, hdc in next ch-1 sp, dc in next 2 dc, skip next st; repeat from ★ 2 times **more**; join with slip st to first tr: 44 sts and 4 corner ch-3 sps.

Rnd 5: Ch 1, sc in same st as joining, 5 sc in next corner ch-3 sp, ★ sc in each st across to next corner ch-3 sp, 5 sc in corner sp; repeat from ★ 2 times **more**, sc in each st across; join with slip st to first sc, finish off: 64 sc.

SQUARE #1 (Make 12)

With Color B, ch 3; join with slip st to form a ring.

Rnd 1 (Right side)**:** Ch 3, 11 dc in ring; join with slip st to first dc: 12 dc.

Note: Mark Rnd 1 as **right** side.

Rnd 2: Ch 4, (dc in next dc, ch 1) 11 times; join with slip st to first dc, finish off: 12 dc and 12 ch-1 sps.

Rnd 3: With **right** side facing, join Color A with dc in same st as joining ***(see Joining With Dc, page 29)***; (dc, ch 1, dc) in next ch-1 sp, ★ dc in next dc, (dc, ch 1, dc) in next ch-1 sp; repeat from ★ around; join with slip st to first dc, finish off: 36 dc and 12 ch-1 sps.

Rnd 4: With **right** side facing, join Color C with slip st in first ch-1 sp after joining; ch 7, tr in same sp, skip next dc, dc in next 2 dc, hdc in next ch-1 sp, sc in next 3 dc, hdc in next ch-1 sp, dc in next

2 dc, skip next dc, ★ (tr, ch 3, tr) in next ch-1 sp, skip next dc, dc in next 2 dc, hdc in next ch-1 sp, sc in next 3 dc, hdc in next ch-1 sp, dc in next 2 dc, skip next st; repeat from ★ 2 times **more**; join with slip st to first tr: 44 sts and 4 corner ch-3 sps.

Rnd 5: Ch 1, sc in same st as joining, 5 sc in next corner ch-3 sp, ★ sc in each st across to next corner ch-3 sp, 5 sc in corner sp; repeat from ★ 2 times **more**, sc in each st across; join with slip st to first sc, finish off: 64 sc.

SQUARE #2 (Make 12)

With Color C, ch 3; join with slip st to form a ring.

Rnd 1 (Right side)**:** Ch 3, 11 dc in ring; join with slip st to first dc: 12 dc.

Note: Mark Rnd 1 as **right** side.

Rnd 2: Ch 4, (dc in next dc, ch 1) 11 times; join with slip st to first dc, finish off: 12 dc and 12 ch-1 sps.

Rnd 3: With **right** side facing, join Color A with dc in same st as joining; (dc, ch 1, dc) in next ch-1 sp, ★ dc in next dc, (dc, ch 1, dc) in next ch-1 sp; repeat from ★ around; join with slip st to first dc, finish off: 36 dc and 12 ch-1 sps.

Rnd 4: With **right** side facing, join Color B with slip st in first ch-1 sp after joining; ch 7, tr in same sp, skip next dc, dc in next 2 dc, hdc in next ch-1 sp, sc in next 3 dc, hdc in next ch-1 sp, dc in next 2 dc, skip next dc, ★ (tr, ch 3, tr) in next ch-1 sp, skip next dc, dc in next 2 dc, hdc in next ch-1 sp, sc in next 3 dc, hdc in next ch-1 sp, dc in next 2 dc, skip next st; repeat from ★ 2 times **more**; join with slip st to first tr: 44 sts and 4 corner ch-3 sps.

Rnd 5: Ch 1, sc in same st as joining, 5 sc in next corner ch-3 sp, ★ sc in each st across to next corner ch-3 sp, 5 sc in corner sp; repeat from ★ 2 times **more**, sc in each st across; join with slip st to first sc, finish off: 64 sc.

ASSEMBLY

With **wrong** sides together and using Placement Diagram as a guide, whipstitch Squares together with Color A *(Fig. 3, page 30)*, forming 4 vertical strips of 12 Squares each, beginning and ending in corner sc; then whipstitch strips together in same manner.

PLACEMENT DIAGRAM

solid square	square #1	solid square	square #1
square #2	solid square	square #2	solid square
solid square	square #1	solid square	square #1
square #2	solid square	square #2	solid square
solid square	square #1	solid square	square #1
square #2	solid square	square #2	solid square
solid square	square #1	solid square	square #1
square #2	solid square	square #2	solid square
solid square	square #1	solid square	square #1
square #2	solid square	square #2	solid square
solid square	square #1	solid square	square #1
square #2	solid square	square #2	solid square

EDGING

Rnd 1: With **right** side of short edge facing, join Color A with sc in center sc of first corner ***(see Joining With Sc, page 29)***; sc in same st, work 64 sc evenly spaced across to center sc of next corner (16 sc per square), 3 sc in center sc, work 192 sc evenly spaced across to center sc of next corner, 3 sc in center sc, work 64 sc evenly spaced across to center sc of next corner, 3 sc in center sc, work 192 sc evenly spaced across, sc in same st as first sc; join with slip st to first sc: 524 sc.

Rnd 2: Ch 1, turn; 2 sc in same st as joining, ★ sc in each sc across to center sc of next corner, 3 sc in center sc; repeat from ★ 2 times **more**, sc in each sc across, sc in same st as first sc; join with slip st to first sc: 532 sc.

Rnd 3: Ch 3, do **not** turn; skip next sc, ★ slip st in next sc, ch 3, skip next sc; repeat from ★ around; join with slip st at base of beginning ch-3, finish off.

General Instructions

ABREVIATIONS

CC	Contrasting Color
ch(s)	chain(s)
cm	centimeters
hdc	half double crochet(s)
dc	double crochet(s)
MC	Main Color
mm	millimeters
Rnd(s)	Round(s)
sc	single crochet(s)
sp(s)	space(s)
st(s)	stitch(es)
tr	treble crochet(s)
YO	yarn over

CROCHET TERMINOLOGY		
UNITED STATES		INTERNATIONAL
slip stitch (slip st)	=	single crochet (sc)
single crochet (sc)	=	double crochet (dc)
half double crochet (hdc)	=	half treble crochet (htr)
double crochet (dc)	=	treble crochet (tr)
treble crochet (tr)	=	double treble crochet (dtr)
double treble crochet (dtr)	=	triple treble crochet (ttr)
triple treble crochet (tr tr)	=	quadruple treble crochet (qtr)
skip	=	miss

SYMBOLS & TERMS

★ — work instructions following ★ as many **more** times as indicated in addition to the first time.

† to † — work all instructions from first † to second † **as many** times as specified.

( ) or [ ] — work enclosed instructions **as many** times as specified by the number immediately following **or** work all enclosed instructions in the stitch or space indicated **or** contains explanatory remarks.

colon (:) — the number given after a colon at the end of a row or round denotes the number of stitches or spaces you should have on that row or round.

BEGINNER	Projects for first-time crocheters using basic stitches. Minimal shaping.
EASY	Projects using yarn with basic stitches, repetitive stitch patterns, simple color changes, and simple shaping and finishing.
INTERMEDIATE	Projects using a variety of techniques, such as basic lace patterns or color patterns, mid-level shaping and finishing.
EXPERIENCED	Projects with intricate stitch patterns, techniques and dimension, such as non-repeating patterns, multi-color techniques, fine threads, small hooks, detailed shaping and refined finishing.

GAUGE

Exact gauge is **essential** for proper size. Before beginning your Shawl, make a sample swatch in the yarn and hook specified in the individual instructions. After completing the swatch, measure it, counting your stitches and rows or rounds carefully. If your swatch is larger or smaller than specified, **make another, changing hook size to get the correct gauge**. Keep trying until you find the size hook that will give you the specified gauge.

JOINING WITH SC

When instructed to join with a sc, begin with a slip knot on the hook. Insert hook in stitch or space indicated, YO and pull up a loop, YO and draw through both loops on hook.

JOINING WITH DC

When instructed to join with a dc, begin with a slip knot on the hook. YO, holding loop on hook, insert hook in stitch or space indicated, YO and pull up a loop (3 loops on hook), (YO and draw through 2 loops on hook) twice.

CROCHET HOOKS																	
U.S.	B-1	C-2	D-3	E-4	F-5	G-6	7	H-8	I-9	J-10	K-10½	L-11	M/N-13	N/P-15	P/Q	Q	S
Metric - mm	2.25	2.75	3.25	3.5	3.75	4	4.5	5	5.5	6	6.5	8	9	10	15	16	19

Yarn Weight Symbol & Names	LACE 0	SUPER FINE 1	FINE 2	LIGHT 3	MEDIUM 4	BULKY 5	SUPER BULKY 6	JUMBO 7
Type of Yarns in Category	Fingering, size 10 crochet thread	Sock, Fingering, Baby	Sport, Baby	DK, Light Worsted	Worsted, Afghan, Aran	Chunky, Craft, Rug	Super Bulky, Roving	Jumbo, Roving
Crochet Gauge* Ranges in Single Crochet to 4" (10 cm)	32-42 sts**	21-32 sts	16-20 sts	12-17 sts	11-14 sts	8-11 sts	6-9 sts	5 sts and fewer
Advised Hook Size Range	Steel*** 6 to 8, Regular hook B-1	B-1 to E-4	E-4 to 7	7 to I-9	I-9 to K-10½	K-10½ to M/N-13	M/N-13 to Q	Q and larger

*GUIDELINES ONLY: The chart above reflects the most commonly used gauges and hook sizes for specific yarn categories.

** Lace weight yarns are usually crocheted with larger hooks to create lacy openwork patterns. Accordingly, a gauge range is difficult to determine. Always follow the gauge stated in your pattern.

*** Steel crochet hooks are sized differently from regular hooks–the higher the number, the smaller the hook, which is the reverse of regular hook sizing.

FREE LOOPS OF A CHAIN

When instructed to work in free loops of a chain, work in loop indicated by arrow ***(Fig. 1)***.

Fig. 1

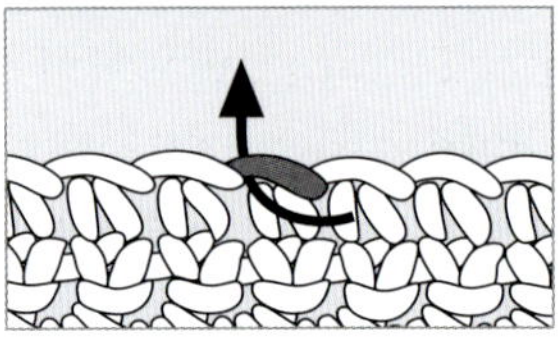

CHANGING COLORS

Work the last stitch to within one step of completion, hook new yarn ***(Figs. 2a & b)*** and draw through both loops on hook.

Fig. 2a

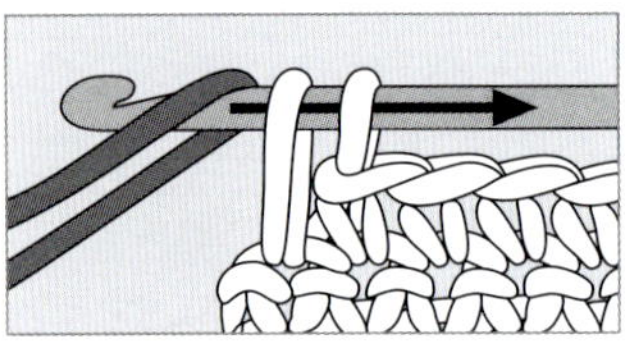

Fig. 2b

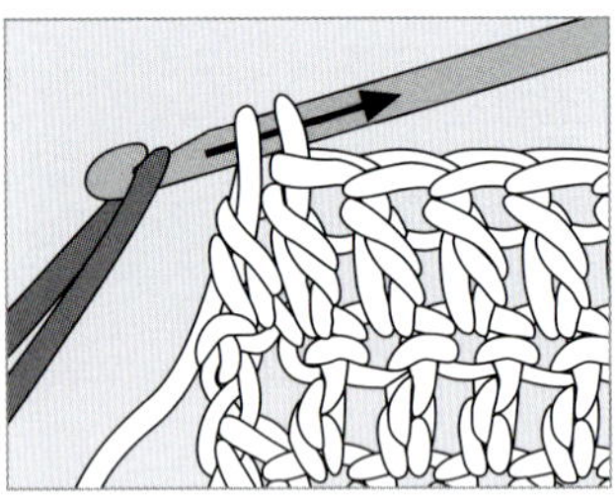

WHIPSTITCH

Place two Squares with **wrong** sides together. Beginning in center sc of corner, sew through both pieces once to secure the beginning of the seam, leaving an ample yarn end to weave in later. Insert the needle from **front** to **back** through **both** loops on **both** pieces ***(Fig. 3)***. Bring the needle around and insert it from **front** to **back** through next loops on both pieces. Continue in this manner across ending in center sc of next corner and keeping the sewing yarn fairly loose.

Fig. 3

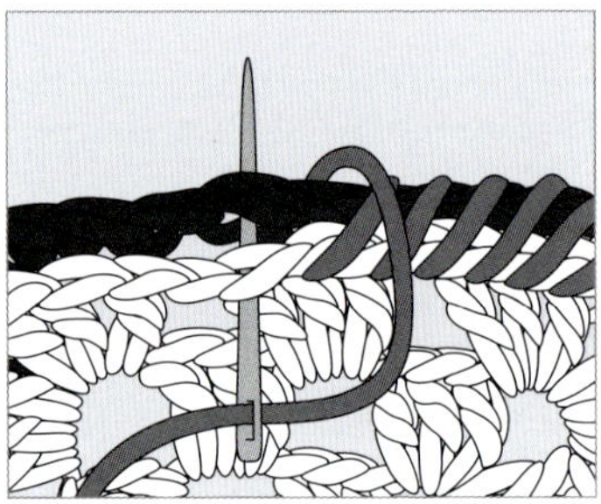

Yarn Information

The Shawls in this book were made using Medium Weight Yarn. Any brand of Medium Weight Yarn may be used. It is best to refer to the yardage/meters when determining how many balls or skeins to purchase. Remember, to arrive at the finished size, it is the GAUGE/TENSION that is important, not the brand of yarn.

For your convenience, listed below are the specific yarn styles and colors used to create our photography models. Because yarn manufacturers make frequent changes in their product lines, you may sometimes find it necessary to use a substitute yarn or to search for the discontinued product at alternate suppliers (locally or online).

GRANNY SQUARE SHAWL
Paton's® Décor™
MC - #87671 Pale Grey Heather
Color A - #87614 Winter White
Color B - #87622 Rich Country Blue
Color C - #87700 Mandarin
Color D - #87438 Rose

HUDSON SHAWL
Caron® Simply Soft®
MC - #9702 Off White
Color A - #9707 Dark Sage
Color B - #9763 Harvest Red
Color C - #9755 Sunshine
Color D - #9727 Black

STRIPES STOLE
Lion Brand® Landscapes®
#206 Metropolis

MEDITATION SHAWL
Lion Brand® Landscapes®
MC - #143 Bordeaux
CC - #140 Rose

PATCHWORK SHAWL
Lion Brand® Heartland®
MC - #125 Mammoth Cave
Color A - #174 Joshua Tree
Color B - #158 Yellowstone
Color C - #122 Grand Canyon

We have made every effort to ensure that these instructions are accurate and complete. We cannot, however, be responsible for human error, typographical mistakes, or variations in individual work.

Production Team: Instructional/Technical Editor - Linda A. Daley; Editorial Writer - Susan Frantz Wiles; Senior Graphic Artist - Lora Puls; Graphic Artist - Victoria Temple; Photo Stylist - Lori Wenger; and Photographer - Jason Masters.